To: _ _ _ _ _ _ _ _

Love: _ _ _ _ _ _

GRANDPARENTS ARE SPECIAL™

A TRIBUTE TO THOSE WHO LOVE, NURTURE, & INSPIRE

COMPILED BY
LUCY MEAD

GRAMERCY BOOKS
NEW YORK

© 2000 by Random House Value Publishing, Inc.

This 2000 edition is published by Gramercy Books™, an imprint of Random House Value Publishing, Inc., 280 Park Avenue, New York, N.Y. 10017

Gramercy Books™ and design are trademarks of Random House Value Publishing, Inc.

Random House
New York • Toronto • London • Sydney • Auckland
http://www.randomhouse.com/

Interior Design: Karen Ocker Design, New York

Printed and bound in Singapore.

Library-of-Congress Cataloging-in-Publication Data

Grandparents are special: a tribute to those who love, encourage, & inspire / compiled by Lucy Mead.
     p. cm.
  ISBN 0-517-16265-2
    1. Grandparents—Quotations, maxims, etc. 2. Grandparents—Anecdotes. 3. Grandparents—Poetry. I. Mead, Lucy.

PN6084.G6 G75 2000
  306.874'5—dc21   00-021802

8 7 6 5 4 3 2 1

GRANDPARENTS
ARE SPECIAL™

If asked their opinions about becoming grannies, a lot of men and women would say, "No thanks, not just yet," for we live in a world where short-skirted grandmas boogie to the best of life and golf-playing grandpas dream of shooting their age.

We are the generation that came of age in an ageless society.

Nobody looks like a grandmother
Nobody feels like a grandfather.
But, ready or not, here come our grandchildren!

LOIS WYSE, *Grandchildren are so much fun I should have had them first*

WE ARE NEVER OLD

Spring still makes spring in the mind
    When sixty years are told;
Love wakes anew this throbbing heart,
    And we are never old;
Over the winter glaciers
    I see the summer glow,
And through the wild-piled snowdrift
    The warm rosebuds below.

RALPH WALDO EMERSON, "The World-Soul"

Don't send your children subscriptions to your local newspaper. Your grandchildren might get a job from the want ads and move in with you.

MARY MCBRIDE, *Grandma Knows Best, But No One Ever Listens!*

Her hair was entirely gray, long and thin, piled in a flat pug on the very top of her head. Her forehead was high, above her round, gold-framed glasses that covered the most expressive, bright, hazel eyes I had ever seen. The flesh over her cheekbones was firm and round and rose colored. Her nose, slightly Roman, was a well-shaped one. Deep lines ran to the base of her round chin and there were two soft packets of flesh that sagged below each side. Her face was patterned with work lines.

BETH MOSES HICKOK, *Remembering Grandma Moses*

Old age is no place for sissies.

BETTE DAVIS

BLESSING FOR GRANDPARENT'S DAY

They are inspiration, Lord of history, having the souls of playmates and wisdom of sages, these grandparents we honor on their special day. Gently wise, they know that like sunflowers ripening in today's autumn glory, children are best supported, not burdened; best encouraged, not reshaped, expecting them only to become all You intend. Bless and keep them, for the grandchildren are growing from their sturdy, life-giving roots.

MARGARET ANNE HUFFMAN
in *Family Celebrations*

My Grandma always used to say,
"Ya gotta get happy in the same
clothes you got mad in."

RON, AGE 43

Never stray from the path, never eat a windfall apple and
never trust a man whose eyebrows meet in the middle.

GRANNY in *The Company of Wolves, 1984*

Grandparents are our continuing tie to the near-past, to
the events and beliefs and experiences that so strongly
affect our lives and the world around us.

JIMMY CARTER, Former U.S. President

Thursdays—my mother's bridge game day—
belonged to Grandpa. Every Thursday he picked
me up at my bus stop and we walked up Central
Park West to the Museum of Natural History.
The choice was mine: The Dinosaurs, North
American Mammals, African Mammals, Gems
and Semi-Precious Stones . . . anything I wanted.
Each week we spent hours in one very special
part of the museum and then went back to his
house where Grandma made me Arnold thin
toast with sweet butter.

ROSE, AGE 52

What children need most are the essentials that
grandparents provide in abundance. They give
unconditional love, kindness, patience, humor, comfort,
lessons in life. And, most importantly, cookies."

RUDOLPH W. GIULIANI, Mayor of New York City

"O.K., I'm not complaining. All I'm saying is this: I'm not
getting any younger. I would like to know before I die that
you are married and happy and not alone in the world. I
would, believe, go into the coffin with a smile on my face to
have seen and held on my lap a couple of grandchildren."

DAN GREENBERG, *How to Be a Jewish Mother*

QUOTES FROM THE
GRANDPARENTS HOT-LINE WEBSITE:

Age is a high price to pay for maturity.

I can remember when the air
was clean and sex was dirty.

If you think health care is expensive now,
wait until you see what it costs when it's free.

The hardest thing in life to learn is which
bridge to cross and which to burn.

The secret of growing old is having lots
of experience you can no longer use.

Nobody can do for little children what
grandparents do. Grandparents sort of sprinkle
stardust over the lives of little children.

ALEX HALEY

Thinking about the grandfather I wish I had prepares me
for the grandfather I wish to be, a way of using what I am
to shape the best that is to come. It is a preparation.

Sometime, not too far from now, a child will call out
"Grandfather," and I will know what to do.

ROBERT FULGHUM,
All I Really Need to Know I Learned in Kindergarten

Growing old is something
you do if you're lucky.

GROUCHO MARX

Grandparents are the solid foundation of
our families and our communities. They root
us in our past with their memories of days
gone by and prepare us for the future with
their ageless wisdom.

TOMMY G. THOMPSON, Governor of Wisconsin

The prosperity of a country is in accordance
with its treatment of the aged.

HASSIDIC SAYING

To be 70 years young is sometimes far more
cheerful and hopeful than to be 40 years old.

OLIVER WENDELL HOLMES, JR.

The person who has lived the most
is not the one with the most years but
the one with the richest experiences.

JEAN JACQUES ROUSSEAU

When the grandmothers of today
hear the word "Chippendales,"
they don't necessarily think of chairs.

JOAN KERR, Comedienne

Does Grandpa love to baby-sit his grandchildren?
Are you kidding? By day he is too busy taking
hormone shots at the doctor's or chip shots on
the golf course. At night he and Grandma are too
busy doing the cha-cha.

HAL BOYLE, American journalist (1911-1974)

Heredity is a strong factor, even in architecture. Necessity
first mothered invention. Now invention has little ones
of her own and they look just like grandma.

E. B. WHITE, author of *Charlotte's Web*

The Queen Mother, with a lifetime's
popularity, seemed incapable of a bad
performance as national grandmother
—warm, smiling, human, understanding,
she embodied everything the public
could want of its grandmother.

JOHN PEARSON, British guitarist

My grandma let's me cook and
she doesn't care if I make a mess.

SALLY McCARTHY, AGE 5

When grandparents enter the door,
discipline flies out the window.

OGDEN NASH

The first cigarette I ever had I smoked behind Grandpa's
barn. It made me dizzy, and I coughed a lot.
   "Don't worry, that always happens with the first one,"
said Grandpa. "Try another one."
And you know, he was right.

JACK HANDEY, *Fuzzy Memories*

TO MY GRANDMOTHER

This Relative of mine
Was she seventy-and-nine
   When she died?
By the canvas may be seen
How she'd look'd at seventeen,
   As a Bride.

With her bridal-wreath bouquet
Lace farthingale, and gay
   Falbala,—
If Romeny's touch be true,
What a lucky dog were you,
   Grandpapa!

That good-for-nothing Time
Has a confidence sublime!
    When I first
Saw this Lady, in my youth,
Her winters had, forsooth,
    Done their worst.

Oh if you now are there,
And sweet as once you were,
    Grandmamma,
This nether world agrees
You'll all the better please
    Grandpapa.

FREDERICK LOCKER LAMPSON, 1862

The handwriting on the wall means
the grandchildren found the crayons.

ANON.

Tennessee woman remembering her Old South Grandmother:

No matter how many new ways and new rules I've learned
traveling to other parts of the country, I still will never
forget the things my grandmother always emphasized. My
favorite is that you should always wear your neckline lower
in the back than you do in the front. It's not the impression
you make, it's the impression you leave.

MARYLN SCHWARTZ, *New Times in the Old South*

Children have never been very good at
listening to their elders, but they have
never failed to imitate them.

JAMES BALDWIN

The closest friends I have made all through life
have been people who also grew up close to a
loved and loving grandmother or grandfather.

MARGARET MEAD

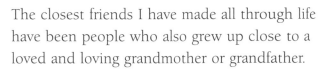

You are old enough to be a grandma if...

When you raise your arm to wave,
the flab underneath waves first.

You decide to find a job and discover the
references on your last resume are all deceased.

The aerobics instructor looks at you when
she says, 'Everybody take a rest.'

You don't care what the dentist says about your
teeth, as long as he says you can keep them.

MARY McBRIDE, *Grandma Knows
Best, But No One Ever Listens!*

The best baby-sitters, of course, are the baby's grandparents. You feel completely comfortable entrusting your baby to them for long periods, which is why most grandparents flee to Florida.

DAVE BARRY, *Babies and Other Hazards of Sex*

In our first week together, Grandma told me it was a sin the way I wasted hot water, toilet paper, my spare time. She said she'd never heard of a girl who had reached my age without learning to crochet. I retaliated by shocking her as best I could. At breakfast, I drowned my scrambled eggs in plugs of ketchup. Evenings, I danced wildly by myself to my 45s while she watched from the doorway.

WALLY LAMB, *She's Come Undone*

Perfect love sometimes does
not come until the first grandchild.

WELSH PROVERB

...a grandmother accompanied with all her family was
celebrating her 90th birthday [in my restaurant] and my
waiters, accompanied with a mechanical organ...were
singing out of tune! At that moment, Paul McCartney
stood up and came next to the grandmother and sang
"Happy Birthday" just for her. When he finished, he just
went back to his table and sat down. Probably nobody
recognized him and certainly not her....I guess he had a
grandmother and wanted to please this lady.

CHEF PAUL BOCUSE

Senescence begins
And middle age ends
The day your descendents
Outnumber your friends.

OGDEN NASH

You know you're getting old when
the candles cost more than the cake.

BOB HOPE

Time and trouble will tame an advanced young woman,
but an advanced old woman is uncontrollable by any
earthly force.

DOROTHY SAYERS

My grandmothers are full of memories
Smelling of soap and onions and wet clay
With veins rolling roughly over quick hands
They have many clean words to say,
My grandmothers were strong.

MARGARET WALKER, "LINEAGE"

Golde: Grandmother Tzeitel! How did she look?

Tevye: For a woman who has been dead for thirty
         years she looked pretty well.

FIDDLER ON THE ROOF, 1971

…nothing can ever take the place of a
child running in and out of your home—
or of a granny's lap to snuggle into.

ROSEMARY WELLS, *"Your Grandchild and You"*

…the Queen Mother listened to Charles's plaintive
outpourings about his loneliness, his homesickness,
the impossibility of blending into school like other
boys… More than either of Charles's parents, perhaps,
his grandmother understood the ordeal of the quiet,
uncertain child in a harsh and alien world.

ANTHONY HOLDEN, *Charles at Fifty*

LAUNDRY ADVICE TO A BRIDE FROM
HER GRANDMOTHER CIRCA 1800

1. bild a fire in back yard to heet kettle of rain water
2. set tubs so smoke won't blow in eyes if wind is pert
3. shave 1 hole cake soap in bilin water
4. sort things—make 2 piles, 1 pile white, 1 pile cullord
5. stur flour in cold water, to smooth, then thin down with bilin water
6. rub dirty spots on board, scrub hard, then bile, rub cullord but don't bile—just rench
7. take white things out of kettle with broom stick handle, then rench, blew, and starch

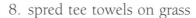

8. spred tee towels on grass

9. hang rags on fence

10. pore rench water in flower bed

11. scrub porch with hot soapy water

12. turn tubs upside down

13. go put on cleen dress—smooth hair with
    side combs—brew cup of tee—set and rest
    and rocka spell and count your blessings.

R. LEWISH BOWMAN, *Bumfuzzled*

GRANNY

Granny's come to our house,
And ho! My lawzy-daisy!
All the children round the place
Is ist a-runnin' crazy!
Fetched a cake fer little Jake,
And fetched a pie fer Nanny,
And fetched a pear fer all the pack
That runs to kiss their Granny!

JAMES WHITCOMB RILEY, 1895

You know you're getting old when you stoop to tie your shoes
and wonder what else you can do while you're down there.

GEORGE BURNS

I'm at an age where my back
goes out more than I do.

PHYLLIS DILLER

She was the grandmother with the dancing eyes who
loved to roller-skate with me, even into her late eighties,
who baked exquisite little cookies, and spoke to the
children in the town where she lived as though they
were grown up and understood her. She was very wise,
and very funny, and they loved her. And if they pressed
her to, she did card tricks for them, which always
fascinated them.

DANIELLE STEEL, *Granny Dan*

I loved their home. Everything smelled
older, worn but safe; the food aroma
had baked itself into the furniture.

SUSAN STRASBERG, "BITTERSWEET"

Why do grandparents and grandchildren get along so
well? They have the same enemy—the mother.

CLAUDETTE COLBERT

If you survive long enough,
you're revered—rather like an old building.

KATHARINE HEPBURN

Among the things that are quite easy,
even simple for a child to operate,
are the grandparents.

JAMES E. MYERS, *A Treasury of Senior Humor*

"A Walrus ate my overcoat and I was freezing to
death. The polar bear saw me shivering with my skin
all blue. He knitted me a sweater with a matching wool
hat, and that's why I'm alive today…"

"Polar Bears can't knit," Molly said.

"Well, that's true, as a rule," said Grampa. "But this
one had worked for a dressmaker in Paris. She loved him
very much and she taught him how to knit sweaters."

ALAN ARKIN, *Some Fine Grampa!*

I don't go along with all this talk of a generation
gap. We're all contemporaries. There is only a
difference in memories, that's all.

W. H. AUDEN

My granddaughter Ava is on the one hand very fragile and
on the other she's very energetic. She wants to be part of
the world real fast. And grandparents very quickly fall in
love with their grandchildren. I think it's that you are on
your way out and they are on their way in. If you look at
it in the extreme, that's what's happening.

PHOTOGRAPHER LEE FRIEDLANDER,
New York Times Magazine interview, 1999

If your baby is "beautiful and perfect, never cries
or fusses, sleeps on schedule and burps on demand,
an angel all the time" . . . You're the grandma.

TERESA BLOOMINGDALE, Columnist

Grandma Lindy Owens…worked all the time trying to
make a better home for her large family and her grandchildren. She took us with her when she hunted plants for
her dyes. She taught us about the wild herbs for medi-
cines and showed us where the spring greens grew. In the
springtime, she would lead us through the woods and tell
us about the plants and their uses and where the wild-
flowers grew.

DOLLY PARTON'S SISTER, WILLADEENE,
in *Smoky Mountain Memories*

From the time I was Alex's [my son's] age,
I would spend every Saturday night with my
grandmother. She'd open her sofa bed for us,
the one that was called a Castro Convertible, and
we'd watch the Million Dollar Movie on television
together. During the commercials, she'd make tea
for me, sweet and pale with milk. Afterward,
I'd fall asleep with the metal bar of the Castro
Convertible pressing into my hip, the sound of
her thunderous snoring in my ears.

JANIS COOKE NEWMAN in *Salon Magazine,* 1999

It doesn't make me feel old to carry pictures of my
grandchildren, but it does make me feel old when
I can't see the pictures without my glasses.

Lois Wyse, *Funny, You Don't Look Like a Grandmother*

Grandmothers already *have* tenure.

A grandmother is a safe haven.

Grandmothers don't *have* to be politically correct.

It's always *safe* to talk to a grandmother.

SUZETTE HADEN ELGIN in *The Grandmother Principle*

It is the nostalgic role of grandmothers to impart affection and love in the way that parents are too busy to do. Ideally, grandmother's house was the place where rules were relaxed and cookies always available. Grandmother was soft and warm while grandfather was gruff and silent. Grandmother let you play with interesting things, old fashioned dresses and shoes, jewelry and hats...A trip to her attic revealed strange treasures, old sewing machines, blanket boxes holding old quilts and trunks full of fashion magazines.

EXHIBITION NOTES TO HISTORICAL TEXTILE
EXHIBITION IN 1998 AT WHYTE MUSEUM
OF THE CANADIAN ROCKIES.

I have always felt that a woman has the right to treat the subject of her age with ambiguity until, perhaps, she passes into the realm of over ninety. Then it is better she be candid with herself and with the world.

HELENA RUBENSTEIN

There's always been a good explanation for every-thing. When that owl attacked Grandma and started biting her head, at first it didn't make any sense. Why would an owl attack Grandma? But then we found out later: a mouse was living in her hairdo.

JACK HANDEY, *Fuzzy Memories*

I'm 65 and I guess that puts me in with
the geriatrics. But if there were fifteen months
in every year, I'd only be 48. That's the trouble
with us. We number everything.

JAMES THURBER

I would drive her [my grandmother's] powder blue
Mercedes for her to wherever we had picked to go to
lunch that day—likely a tearoom. She liked tearooms
best for lunch. I'd go along willingly, because I enjoyed
the delicate kind of food they served, even though
I always felt ungainly sitting at one of her fancy
tearoom tables.

GRAYSON HURST DAUGHTERS in *Salon Magazine, 1998*

I've even had trouble concocting a properly grandmotherish alias . . . After careful consideration, I've decided Ono is appropriate. It's short, easily pronounceable, and was the first thing I said in response to my daughter's "Guess what! We're going to have a BABY!"

SUZANN LEDBETTER, *The Toast Always Lands Jelly-Side Down*

Because [grandparents] are usually free to love and guide and befriend the young without having to take daily responsibility for them, they can often reach out past pride and fear of failure and close the space between generations.

JIMMY CARTER, Former U.S. President

Old age is like a plane flying
through a storm. Once you're aboard,
there's nothing you can do.

GOLDA MEIR

My grandfather, who owned three retail men's
stores, had a reputation as a great salesman.
So great, in fact, that people still talk about the
time he sold a woman a funeral suit for her
husband with an extra pair of pants.

REGINA, AGE 85

By your grandchild you are cherished.
Your words are heard with awe.
But to your grandchild's parent,
You're just a mother-in-law.

MARY MCBRIDE, *Grandma Knows*
Best, But No One Ever Listens!

I used to be with it, then they changed what
it was. Now what was it isn't it, and what is it is
weird and scary to me. I'll happen to you too.

GRANDPA SIMPSON in *The Simpsons*

Modern invention has banished the spinning wheel,
and the same law of progress makes the woman of
today a different woman from her grandmother.

SUSAN B. ANTHONY

If a child is to keep alive his inborn sense of wonder
without any such gift from the fairies, he needs the
companionship of at least one adult who can share it,
rediscovering with him the joy, excitement, and mystery
of the world we live in.

RACHEL CARSON, *I've got a special friend*

If I hadn't started painting,
I would have raised chickens.

GRANDMA MOSES

My grandfather was a very tall man; I had to reach up to hold his hand while walking. He wore dark blue and gray herringbone suits, and the coat flap was a long way up, the gold watch chain almost out of sight. I could see his walking cane moving opposite me, briskly swung with the rhythm of his stride: it was my companion.

ELIZABETH SPENCER, *Landscapes of the Heart*

My grandmother Ernestine Dale enjoyed absolutely *nothing* as far as I could see, except television; Daddy had bought them the first set in town. Grandmother claimed to watch only the quiz shows, calling them "educational," but in fact she watched that television all the time. She had trained Aunt Chloe to hop up and turn it off the moment a visitor arrived on the porch; by the time Aunt Chloe had let the visitor into the parlor, my grandmother would be reading the *Upper Room* or the Bible.

LEE SMITH, *News of the Spirit*

The only one that really loved me was my grandmother, Bubeh. Bubeh loved me. Bubeh was a warm, funny woman who spoke no English and was full of life. She was heavy and short, and after she had been here awhile she did away with that wig she wore in Europe and wore her long, shiny white hair combed and twisted into a found bun on the top of her head. She was clean as a whistle. Clean, I mean, she ironed herself to death. Everything she wore was cleaned and ironed. Her cotton housedresses were freshly washed and ironed.

RUTH MCBRIDE JORDAN, *The Color of Water*

…her [grandchildren] couldn't defeat her. Or
disappoint her. Or prove anything—anything good
or bad—about her. And I saw her free of ambition,
free of the need to control, free of anxiety. Free,
as she liked to put it—to enjoy.

JUDITH VIORST

My grandfather once told me that there were two kinds of
people: those who do the work and those who take the
credit. He told me to try to be in the first group; there was
much less competition.

INDIRA GANDHI

Grandma had brought a change of clothes in a brown paper bag and her box of snuff that she always used. The dresses she wore were usually orchid or brown and they all had long sleeves. She was the image of neatness. Her auburn hair was pulled back in a soft bun at the back of her head. Grandma was a quiet, gentle lady, often smiling, but I never heard her laugh out loud; and her dark brown eyes held just a hint of some secret sadness that never showed itself.

DOLLY PARTON'S SISTER, WILLADEENE
in Smoky Mountain Memories

An old woman with the soul of a young girl who opened her heart to me, because she felt we were kindred spirits.

She recreated the world, making it a wonderful place in which everything might happen. In which a tree or a stone was so much more than what we could see with our eyes. She showed me how the veins in leaves were alive and pulsating. And she was the first to tell me that plants cried out when you hurt them.

Liv Ullmann, "Changing"

A grandfather is a man who can't understand how his idiot son has such brilliant children.

Milton Berle, *Milton Berle's Private Joke File*

I was her little shadow, and that was just the way I
wanted it. Goggy was two hundred years old and
would let me chase her all around the big old house
and tickle her. When I caught her, I didn't tickle her
too hard because she could've broken.

CAROL BURNETT

I grasped her hand like a common consoling friend
and felt, immediately, the grim forbidding strength
of her, undiminished all these years.

LOUISE ERDRICH

[My grandmother] was the one member of my immediate family who most understood me, or so I thought at the time. Looking back, I think it was not so much her understanding as it was the sheer force of her encouragement that helped me through those years...

LINDA SUNSHINE, "To Grandmother with Love"

Her manner of storytelling evoked tenderness and mystery as she put her face close to mine and fixed me with her big, believing eyes. Thus was the strength that was developing in me directly infused from her.

MAXIM GORKY

Grandaddy used to handle snakes in church,
Granny drank strychnine. I guess you could
say I had a leg up, genetically speaking.

MAX CADY *in Cape Fear* (1991)

The history of our grandparents is remembered not with
rose petals but in the laughter and tears of their children
and their children's children. It is into us that the lives of
grandparents have gone. It is in us that their history
becomes a future.

CHARLES & ANN MORSE,
"Let This Be a Day for Grandparents"

We should all have one person who knows
how to less us despite the evidence,
Grandmother was that a person to me...

PHYLLIS THEROUX

Wiser men than I have thought about age and have never
figured out anything to do except say, "Happy birthday."
What, after all, *is* old. To a child of seven, ten is old; and
to a child of ten, twenty-five is middle aged and fifty is an
archaeological exhibit. And to me, a man of seventy
is...what I want to be, weighing 195, playing tennis with
convalescents, and hearing well enough to hear one of
my grandchildren sweetly say, "Grandpa, was 'The Cosby
Show' anything like 'I Love Lucy'?"

BILL COSBY, Time Flies

You know you're getting old when all the names
in your black book have M.D. after them.

ARNOLD PALMER

When
a child cries for a cookie,
The Mother Is the One Who
puts her foot down and says sternly, "No. You have
already had enough sweets today. You are allowed
a nutritional snack instead. Here's a peach."
The Grandmother Is the One Who
puts an arm around the child and murmurs, "Don't
cry. Here are two cookies because I love you so much."

LOIS WYSE, *Grandchildren are so much*
fun I should have had them first

The joy of being older is that in one's life one can,
towards the end of the run, overact appallingly.

QUENTIN CRISP

The drugstore was a wonderful place. Grandmother and
Grandfather lived upstairs in a warm apartment always
bathed in the rich aroma of German cookies and with
melodies a little lighter than Wagner spilling from the
windup Victrola. They didn't have a phone, and when
Grandmother received a call on the drugstore instrument,
Grandfather summoned her by tapping on the ceiling with
a long pole. She called him to meals by pounding on the
floor with an old wood potato masher.

WALTER CRONKITE, *A Reporter's Life*

". . . Karen's here," my mother says.

"Where?"

"Right here," I say.

"You don't look like Karen."

"Maybe youíre remembering me when I was little.
And besides, I'm wearing a hat."

"I don't recognize you."

"I recognized you right away, Grandma."

"You did? That's good. How are you?"

"Oh, Iím fine."

"Well, I wish I was fine. Then we'd all be fine together."

KAREN BRODINE, "HERE, TAKE MY WORDS,"
When I Am An Old Woman I Shall Wear Purple

He was quite a trumpeter, my grandfather.
His band came to be in a big demand at
bar mitzvahs. For an Italian, Papa John sure
could play Hava Nagilah great.

NADJA SALERNO-SONNENBERG, Violinist, *Nadja On My Way*

I thought the world was manageable—a habit of mind absorbed from my grandmother. With her own peculiar style, Granny managed her small realm according to its necessities, abolishing whatever didn't apply. After Daddy came home from the Navy, Granny's diary reads as though the Pacific war never existed. She had patching to do, grapes to seed for jelly, and peaches to work up. Chickens to kill.

BOBBIE ANN MASON, *Clear Springs: A Memoir*

Why can't we build orphanages next to homes
for the elderly? If someone's sitting in a rocker,
it won't be long before a kid will be in his lap.

CLORIS LEACHMAN in Good Housekeeping

"Grandma, I don't want to get my face washed.
Please don't."

"Every little girl needs to have her face washed
when she gets up of a morning, dear. Then she
should wash three times a day in addition.
I've always done that."

"Yeah! Sure! And just see how your face shrunk!"

JAMES E. MYERS, A Treasury of Senior Humor

"You are old, father William," the young man said,
    "And your hair has become very white;
And yet you incessantly stand on your head—
    Do you think, at your age, it is right?"

"In my youth," father William replied to his son,
    "I feared it might injure the brain;
But, now that I'm perfectly sure I have none,
    Why, I do it again and again."

LEWIS CARROLL

He's a great granddad . . . My kids just love
Grandpa Arnold. . . .They love Grandpa Arnold
because he gives them presents.

STEVEN SPIELBERG, *LIFE* Interview, 1999

Somehow, I have the feeling that if a grandfather became an astronaut, on his return, the grandchildren would ask, "What did you bring us?"

MILTON BERLE, *Milton Berle's Private Joke File*

Papa says, "Get ready for bed and brush your teeth."
Mama says, "Time to clean up."
Grandma reads me stories and gives me ice cream. I like to stay all night with Grandma.

ANNA HINES, *Grandma Gets Grumpy*

. . . There was so much to teach them about life and so little time. I wanted to show my grandson how to bluff his way out of an inside straight. I wanted to take my granddaughter to the mall and dress up like dance hall girls in a saloon and have our pictures taken together in a little booth.

I wanted people to stop me in a supermarket and say, "Your baby is beautiful!" and I would fan myself with a pound of bacon and protest, "Oh puleeese, I'm the grandmother."

ERMA BOMBECK,
A Marriage Made in Heaven or Too Tired for an Affair